The Arctic

ENDANGERED PEOPLE & PLACES

The Arctic

BY DAVID ROOTES

Photographs by Bryan and Cherry Alexander

Lerner Publications Company • Minneapolis

All words that appear in **bold** are explained in the glossary that begins on page 46.

Maps by European Map Graphics Ltd. Photograph on p. 38 courtesy of National Air and Space Administration; all other photographs by Bryan and Cherry Alexander.

This edition first published in the United States in 1996 by Lerner Publications Company, 241 First Avenue North, Minneapolis, MN 55401. Copyright © 1995 Cherrytree Press Ltd.

Library of Congress Cataloging-in-Publication Data
Rootes, David.
    The Arctic / by David Rootes.
      p. cm. — (Endangered people and places)
    Includes index.
    Summary: Discusses life in this harsh habitat, the people, the mineral wealth, and the abuses which threaten its future.
    ISBN 0-8225-2776-6 (lib. bdg. : alk. paper)
    1. Human ecology—Arctic regions—Juvenile literature. 2. Arctic peoples—Juvenile literature. [1. Arctic regions.] I. Alexander, Bryan, ill. II. Alexander, Cherry, ill. III. Title. IV. Series.
GF891.R66 1996
33.73—dc20
                         95-40717
                          CIP
                           AC

Printed in Italy by L.E.G.O. s.p.a., Vicenza
Bound in the United States of America
1 2 3 4 5 6 01 00 99 98 97 96

CONTENTS

LIVING IN THE ARCTIC

Frozen Deserts

Ice caps cover each end of the globe. If you could see them from space, you would be dazzled by their brightness as they reflect the sunlight. Most of the earth's fresh water is frozen in these ice caps. Yet they are as dry as deserts. The ice caps cool the oceans and influence the weather.

The earth spins as it hurtles through space. The planet, which is not completely upright, tilts slightly on its axis (an imaginary line through the center of the earth). At each end of the axis are the earth's poles. The area around the North Pole is called the **Arctic. Antarctica** is the continent surrounding the South Pole. Only scientists, explorers, and a few tourists live there.

The Arctic consists of the huge Arctic Ocean—most of which is covered by ice—and treeless, frozen land. The southern edge of the Arctic is marked by a broad belt of forests, which stretches around the globe.

Despite fierce winds, snowstorms, and freezing temperatures, people have lived in the Arctic for more than 20,000 years. During the last 200 years, their way of life has been changed by the arrival of explorers, traders, and **missionaries** from other lands. This book looks at the people who live in the harsh Arctic wilderness, how they survive, and how their land has changed.

INUIT OR ESKIMO?

Many different groups of people live in the Arctic. Each group has its own customs, lifestyle, and language. Together they are called indigenous (or Native) Arctic peoples.

One North American Arctic group is the Inuit, which means "the people." One person is called an Inuk. The Inuit used to be known as Eskimos, an Algonquian Indian word meaning "eaters of raw meat."

Below: The Sami, who live in Lapland (a region of northern Europe), have colorful traditional costumes.

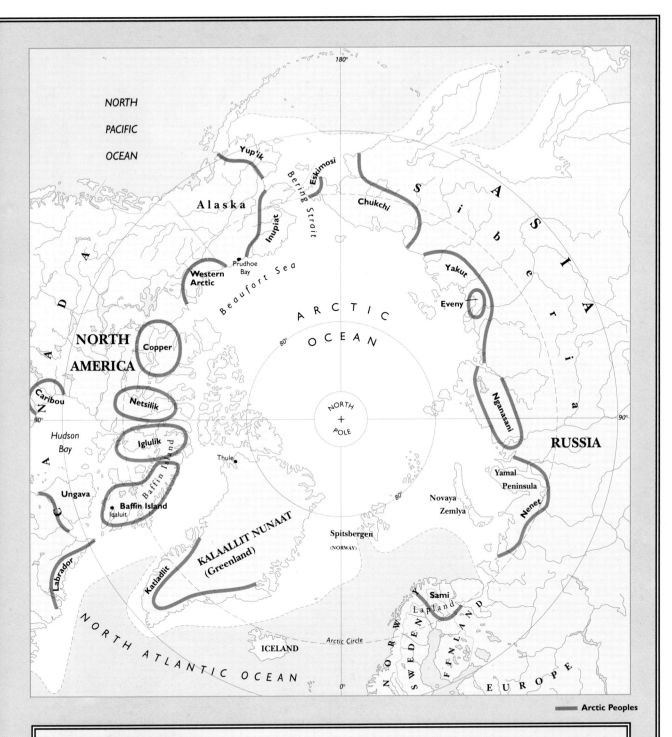

NORTH PACIFIC OCEAN

Yup'ik

Eskimosi

Bering Strait

Chukchi

S I B E R I A

Alaska

Inupiat

Yakut

Prudhoe Bay

Eveny

Western Arctic

Beaufort Sea

A R C T I C

O C E A N

80°

Nganasani

NORTH POLE +

Copper

NORTH AMERICA

Caribou

90°

Netsilik

Hudson Bay

Iglulik

Thule

Baffin Island

Baffin Island

Iqaluit

Ungava

Yamal Peninsula

RUSSIA

Novaya Zemlya

80°

90°

Nenet

KALAALLIT NUNAAT (Greenland)

Spitsbergen

(NORWAY)

Katladlit

Labrador

Sami

Lapland

N O R T H   A T L A N T I C   O C E A N

Arctic Circle

ICELAND

N O R W A Y

S W E D E N

F I N L A N D

E U R O P E

0°

▬▬▬ Arctic Peoples

Latitude and Longitude

Mapmakers have divided up the earth's surface with lines of **latitude,** which circle the globe. Latitude ranges from 0° to 90°, with the **equator** at 0°. Latitude increases from the equator to the poles. Places north of the equator have a north latitude. Those to the south have a south latitude.

Lines of **longitude** run from the North Pole to the South Pole. The zero line passes through a part of London, England, called Greenwich. Lines of longitude are east or west of Greenwich and range from 1° to 180°. The map above is centered on the North Pole.

A FROZEN LAND

Life in the Arctic is difficult. For most of the year, snow covers the ground. In winter every stream and river freezes. Even the sea freezes over. In summer much of the snow melts. But most of the ground below remains frozen and trees cannot grow. At first the only people to visit the Arctic were those who lived in the forests and plains to the south. These hunters came during the short Arctic summer to track the region's animals and birds. Eventually people developed skills that allowed them to stay in the Arctic year-round.

Forest and Tundra

Vast forests border the southern boundary of the Arctic. They stretch across North America and from northern Europe to northern Asia. The people who once lived in these forests used the trees for shelter and firewood. As they learned how to survive the harsh Arctic weather, they were able to live in the region.

According to many geographers, the Arctic begins at the **tree line,** north of which trees do not grow. In North

Above: Many modern Inuit still hunt for some of their food. In winter, when snow and ice cover the ground and the sea, they travel great distances on snowmobiles. Sometimes they use husky dogs to pull sledges. The Inuit invented a type of sled called a sledge (pictured above), which is found nowhere else in the world.

WHERE ARCTIC PEOPLE LIVE

The Sami, or Lapps, live in a region called Lapland, which stretches across northern Norway, Sweden, Finland, and part of Russia. The Sami herd reindeer. The Nenet, another group of herders, inhabit the Yamal Peninsula in Russia. The Chukchi are a people who live farther to the east, near Alaska. This group is more closely related to the Arctic peoples of Alaska than to the Sami or the Nenet.

The Inuit live in the Arctic region of North America. Historically Inuit were hunters, who tracked caribou, caught fish, and hunted sea **mammals** such as seals, walrus, and whales. Inuit live in Greenland, northern Canada, and Alaska.

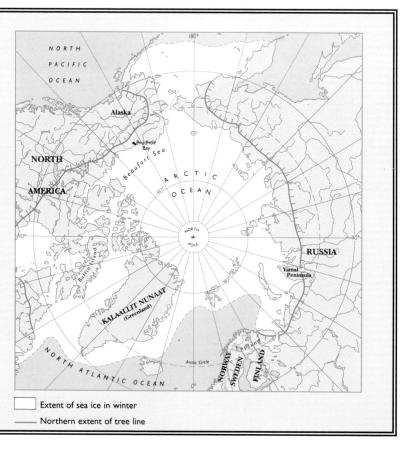

Extent of sea ice in winter

Northern extent of tree line

America, the tree line is far to the south of the Arctic Ocean. When ancient hunters headed north from sheltering forests, they had to travel long distances across the **tundra** (flat, open land), where a strong blizzard could mean death. In northern Europe and Russia, the tree line is much closer to the Arctic Ocean. People could travel north more easily and return to the forests when winter approached.

Arctic Herders

Reindeer and **caribou** are closely related animals. Reindeer live in the far north of Europe, Asia, and North America. Caribou live only in far northern regions of North America. Over time the peoples of Europe and Russia grew to depend on herding reindeer. This way of life is still determined by the **migration** patterns of reindeer herds. In spring herders travel north, following their reindeer to fresh pastures. In fall the herders and animals return south to the shelter of the forests. Between 600,000 and 700,000 people from different groups across northern Europe and Russia still live this way.

Below: This Sami woman is tending reindeer in Norway. In her hand, she is carrying a reindeer antler. Inuit hunters track caribou across the tundra. In summer, these animals migrate (or travel) vast distances searching for grasses, **mosses,** and **lichens** to eat.

UNDERSTANDING THE ARCTIC

Why is the Arctic so cold? One reason is that polar ice caps act like giant mirrors. They reflect much of the sun's light back into space. In the Arctic, the sun sits low in the sky, shining too weakly to have much warmth. Antarctica is even colder than the Arctic. The coldest temperature on earth, –128° F (–90° C), was recorded in Antarctica.

The amount of sea ice in the Arctic Ocean changes during the year. Large areas melt in summer but rapidly freeze again in winter. In the coldest years, sea ice extends from the Bering Strait to the southern tip of Greenland.

Some of the land surrounding the Arctic Ocean is so cold that it is permanently covered by ice. Greenland has a vast ice cap, and **glaciers** flow across parts of Alaska, Canada, and the islands of Spitsbergen. Much of the ground is frozen year-round and is known as **permafrost.** Snow can fall at any time of year. Winter storms blow snow into drifts that look like sand dunes.

The animals and plants of the Arctic have adapted (or, developed) to survive in extremely harsh conditions. Arctic winters last about nine months. During the short summers, much of the snow melts. In some spots, the temperature may climb to 86° F (30° C).

Right: The Arctic is too cold and dry for trees to grow. The open, windswept plains in the Arctic are known as tundra. Many animals spend part of the year in the Arctic tundra, migrating south to forested areas for shelter during the winter.

Right: Permafrost (permanently frozen ground) is a mixture of ice and rock. The surface snow that melts in summer does not seep into the ground because the earth below is frozen. So during the warm months, ponds and rivers form all across the tundra.

Above: Ocean currents and strong winds have shaped this **iceberg.** Icebergs are huge masses of ice that break off the end of glaciers that reach the sea.

SEASONS IN THE ARCTIC

The first sign of spring in the Arctic is the arrival of millions of ducks, geese, and a variety of smaller birds such as arctic terns and golden plovers. These birds fly to the Arctic to breed and raise their young. Many will have traveled thousands of miles from as far away as South America, Africa, or even Antarctica.

Below: Musk oxen stay in the Arctic all year. They provide a source of winter food for some Inuit families. But in the 1800s, whalers hunted the animals to **extinction** in parts of Alaska. When attacked, musk oxen sometimes form a circle, with the adults facing outward protecting the young in the middle.

Summer Plenty

During the warm months, caribou migrate north to the tundra to breed and raise their young. They also come to feed on tundra plants, which grow rapidly during the Arctic summer. Thousands of insects appear. Lemmings, hares, and many other small mammals come out of their winter shelters.

Historically the Inuit moved out of their winter homes during the summer. During this time of plenty, families would dry or bury food to store for the winter.

The Arctic summer is very short. When fall arrives, almost all of the birds head south to spend the winter in warmer climates. Only a few kinds of birds, including ravens, snowy owls, and gyrfalcons, spend the long winter in the Arctic.

Life in the Arctic Ocean

Life in the sea is easier. Land temperatures may drop to –58° F (–50° C) in winter. But the temperature of the ocean, which varies by only a few degrees, is never colder than 28° F (–2° C). At that temperature, sea ice forms

Above: Walrus bask on the shore on a warm summer day. In the 1800s, whalers killed large numbers of walrus for their oil, leaving the Inuit without a valuable source of meat.

Left: Each spring the tundra comes alive with thousands of small, colorful flowers. Insects swarm over the moss. Inuit historically used the dried seed heads of some grasses to line their sealskin boots.

on the surface and insulates the water below so that it does not get any colder.

The Arctic Ocean is full of life year-round. Some ocean animals migrate. For example, whales swim north to feed on **plankton** (small ocean plants and animals), which begin to grow when the sea ice melts in spring. During this season, salmon swim up rivers to spawn, or lay their eggs. They must return downriver to the ocean before the Arctic waters start to freeze over again at the end of summer.

BEATING THE COLD

Many animals stay in the Arctic during the winter. To save energy, some animals hibernate (or, go into a deep sleep) through the coldest weather. Other animals stay active. They find ways to beat the cold, even when everything is covered with snow.

During winter the vital organs of insects temporarily slow down. You might think any liquid inside the insects would freeze and kill the bugs. But scientists have discovered that many cold-climate insects have a sort of antifreeze in their bodies, which prevents their bodies from freezing.

Right: Polar bears hunt seals on the pack ice, especially in spring when seal pups are born. When the bears can't find enough seals, they hunt on land and are a danger to people.

Below: A mother harp seal encourages her pup to join her in the water. Most seal pups are born on sea ice in the spring.

Polar land mammals have a thick covering of fur that holds in heat. Underneath the skin are layers of fat, which also help keep the animals warm. Sometimes spring comes late and snow remains on the ground longer than usual. If this happens, some animals die because they can't find enough food to replace the energy-producing fat they have lost during the winter.

Polar bears give birth during winter. In October pregnant females dig out a den in a deep snowbank, where they bear their young. The mother and her cubs stay in the snow den until March. Seals bear their young in late winter or early spring. Some seals make a den on the sea ice. Most give birth on the surface of the ice, where they may be exposed to harsh weather.

The smallest mammals, such as mice and lemmings, stay active in winter by living underneath the snow. They dig burrows in the ground and eat any roots and shoots they can find. The layers of snow above their burrows protect the animals from the cold.

In winter the temperature of the sea is warmer than the temperature of the air. But animals that live in water lose heat 30 times faster than land animals do. So seals and whales have a thick layer of fat called **blubber,** which helps keep them warm. Many Inuit like to eat muktuk, a layer of whale skin and blubber.

Above: An eider duck lines its nest with fine feathers called down, which helps to keep the eggs warm. In fact, down is so warm that it is collected to fill bedspreads. This is where the name for an eiderdown quilt comes from.

ARCTIC PEOPLES

Scientists studying the Arctic have found traces there of some of the world's earliest humans. These early peoples were hunters, who tracked large animals known as mammoths. Families lived in simple shelters and built fires to keep warm. They lived during a time when the climate was probably warmer than it is now.

The Ice Age

About 20,000 years ago, during the last **Ice Age,** the world's climate was extremely cold, like a permanent winter. Rivers of snow and ice, called glaciers, spread across the land. Over hundreds of years, the glaciers grew and formed ice caps. Most of North America, Europe, and Russia was covered in ice.

Shallow seas dried out because so much water was frozen in the ice caps. One of these dried-out seas was the Bering Strait, a narrow channel of water that separates North America from Asia. During the Ice Age, scientists think that people and animals traveled between the two continents across the land bridge formed by the dried-out strait. Some of the earliest Arctic peoples of North America came across this land bridge.

Right: This Inuk's warm clothing keeps out wind and snow. The first northern people to sew furs together for clothes are known as the Arctic Small Tool Culture. Nowadays some Inuit still use similar materials and methods to make their clothing.

ARCTIC PEOPLES OF THE PAST

One group of people who crossed the land bridge into Arctic North America about 5,000 years ago is known as the Arctic Small Tool Culture. These people hunted small sea mammals such as seals. They also tracked caribou and musk oxen. From walrus tusks and animal bones, they made small tools such as sewing needles, spear and **harpoon** tips, and bone scrapers for cleaning animal skins. The Arctic Small Tool people are also known for the small carvings of animals they left behind.

A group known as the Dorset Culture developed from the Arctic Small Tool people. The Dorsets invented small boats called **kayaks** for hunting at sea. They sewed animal skins into weatherproof clothing so they could hunt all year.

In about A.D. 1000, the Thule Culture spread across North America from Alaska to the east coast of Greenland. The Thule used dogs to pull sledges, which allowed this group to live almost anywhere in the Arctic. The Thule are the direct ancestors of the modern Inuit.

Right: The people of the Arctic Small Tool Culture were named for the tiny tools and carvings they made. This ivory carving of a seal is just a few inches long.

Left: Thousands of tons of water are frozen in the ice caps and glaciers of the Arctic. During the last Ice Age, ice caps spread deep into the heart of Europe, Russia, and North America. Nowadays only Greenland has a thick ice cap, although glaciers cover many other parts of the Arctic.

LIVING WITH COLD

The Inuit had to be creative to survive on the tundra, where wood is not available for making fires or building homes. The frozen landscape makes digging for useful metals extremely difficult. Because the Arctic has so few natural resources, the Inuit learned to take advantage of any materials they could find. They used large bones for making sledges and building some of their dwellings. Stone, ivory, and small bones were crafted into tools.

Inuit relied on various materials for making dwellings to keep warm and to provide shelter from harsh storms.

KAYAKS AND UMIAKS

Inuit relied on two types of boat. Kayaks *(right)* were used for hunting seals and small whales among the **pack ice.** Kayaks are light enough to be carried by one person. On top of the small boat, hunters tied all the equipment they would need, including a harpoon, knife, and lance. To hunt larger whales, Inuit used a bigger boat called an **umiak.** Women often rowed umiaks, which were up to 30 feet (9 meters) long and could carry eight or ten people.

Thule Culture people were the first to hunt regularly at sea. With no wood or metal, they used animal bones and skins to make boats and sledges.

Above: To catch a seal, an Inuk hunter sets a net around a breathing hole. Seals come up for air at these holes in the ice. The animals swim between the holes when they are hunting for their food. When the seal surfaces to breath at this hole, it will become trapped in the net.

This breathing hole lies near an iceberg that is frozen into the winter sea ice. The hunter must be very quiet, since any noise will scare the seal away.

Another way to catch a seal is to harpoon the animal as it surfaces (see page 33). The hunter wears fur clothes to keep warm in the cold. He may have to wait for hours for his catch.

When traveling they carved blocks of snow to build temporary lodgings called **snowhouses.** Snowhouses can be made wherever the right type of snow can be found.

The Inuit constructed more permanent houses partly underground. Inuit builders would dig a pit and form the upper walls and roof from stones and bones. Then they would pile moss turf on top. For a window, Inuit stretched a piece of seal or walrus bladder across a hole in the wall. They burned whale and seal blubber in small soapstone lamps called *kudlik,* which provided heat and light inside the homes. One side of the pit had a raised platform so Inuit could sleep off the cold floor. This platform and the walls were lined with sealskins. People stripped off most of their clothes when they came inside.

Inuit sewed their clothing from a variety of different furs and skins. The warmest winter clothing was made from caribou skin, which also provided a thick sleeping pad. The materials for underclothing came from the skins of young caribou and fox, and sometimes bird skins. The fur trim on the hood of an anorak (jacket) was usually made from wolverine or wolf fur. Nowadays some Inuit still use animal furs and skins to sew traditional clothing.

Specially treated sealskins are almost waterproof. If the seams are sewn with **sinew,** which swells when it is wet, the joints are also waterproof. In some ways, traditional Inuit clothing is better than modern clothing, although it needs constant care to stay in good condition.

Above: Half-buried turf houses provided warm shelters. They were solid enough to withstand fierce blizzards. When the inside became too dirty from continuous use, another house was built.

Below: Snowhouses were made from blocks of snow piled on top of one another. The joints were packed with snow to keep out the wind. Inside, snowhouses are warm and comfortable.

LIVING OFF THE LAND

The Inuit call their harsh Arctic homeland Nunatsiaq, "the beautiful land." The Arctic, however, is not rich in wildlife, and the climate is so cold that crops won't grow. Arctic peoples have had to learn how to make the best from a land where the food supply has always been very limited. Nowadays much of the food people eat is shipped to the Arctic from cities to the south.

Some Native Arctic peoples lead a more **nomadic lifestyle** than others. In northern Russia, for example, the Nenet, Chukchi, and other herders follow the yearly reindeer migration. The Russian herders have learned not to waste scarce resources. They live in the forests some of the time, so they have wood for fuel and building. The population of Russian herders is small, and they are spread out over a very large area. Except for Antarctica, not many places in the world have so few people living there.

Right: Before people could live permanently in the Arctic, they had to find ways to make clothing and shelters that would keep out wind and snow. Crafting needles out of animal bones, the first Arctic peoples were able to sew skins together to make tents and fur clothing such as these modern herders are using.

Below: This Nenet family is taking a break for tea and raw meat while their reindeer graze. Reindeer are kept for their meat, skins, and milk. The animals feed on lichens and grasses. If they stay in one place for too long, they will overgraze and trample the pasture. Some herds travel long distances to find fresh grazing land.

In spring many herders lead their reindeer to pastures on the tundra. In fall they return to the forests to find shelter from winter storms.

LAND OF THE MIDNIGHT SUN

At the equator, every day has 12 hours of daylight and 12 hours of darkness—summer and winter. At the North Pole, daylight is continuous in summer because the sun does not drop below the horizon for six months. In winter the sun does not rise at the North Pole, and the region has six months of night.

Places between the equator and the North Pole have differing amounts of light and dark during the year. The **Arctic Circle** loops the globe at about the 66th parallel of northern latitude. The circle marks the point at which the sun does not set on the longest day of summer (June 21) and does not rise on the shortest day of winter (December 21). People living north of the Arctic Circle will see the sun at midnight at least one day a year.

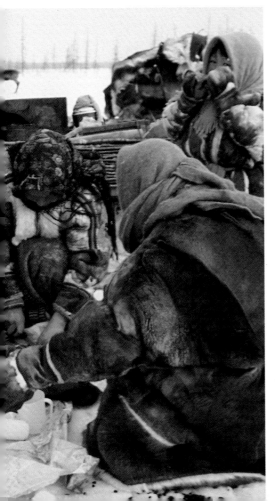

Inuit hunters traveled thousands of miles each year. They searched the frozen ocean and shoreline for seals and polar bears. On land they hunted many different animals.

The Caribou and Its Uses

The caribou has been called the department store of the Inuit. The meat was an important source of food, and Inuit families ate every possible part. Caribou skins were traditionally used to make clothing, tents, and bedding. Caribou antlers were carved into harpoons, and the animals' bones were crafted into tools, building materials, and needles. Thread was made from caribou sinews.

The Inuit invented a type of sledge that is not found anywhere else in the world. Inuit hunters depended heavily on huskies to pull the sledges. In summer, when the sea ice melts, Inuit traveled by kayaks made from sealskin and bones or driftwood.

ANGAKOQ—THE SHAMAN

Why is one hunter lucky and another one comes home empty-handed? Traditional Inuit spiritual beliefs are based on the idea that life is influenced by spirits that live in people, animals, and mysterious monsters. A person's relationship with animals and the land is ruled by this spirit world. If a hunter breaks taboos (rules) while hunting, the animal spirits will become angry. This may mean the hunter will never catch another animal. And if the animal spirits are badly upset, the hunter's entire community could be cursed.

Between the Inuit and the world of spirits is a special healer, known as an **angákoq,** or shaman. If a hunter has bad luck hunting, the shaman will show the hunter how to win favor with the animal spirits. According to traditional Inuit belief, the animal most like the Inuit is the polar bear. Like humans, bears often walk upright and in spring they hunt on the sea ice. Inuit culture has many stories and taboos about polar bears.

TUPILAK

These miniature monsters were often carved from ivory. They were supposed to bring to life the real tupilak—a spirit that could harm an enemy.

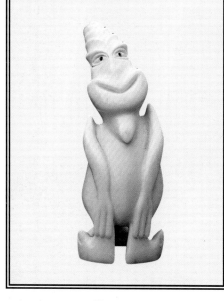

People of the Dorset Culture believed that the shaman had to fly away in a trance to soothe spirits who were angry. The Dorsets made little carvings of polar bears to help the shaman fly.

Inuit often traveled on their own, but they rarely felt alone. According to traditional beliefs, Inuit are accompanied by mischievous spirits that cannot be trusted. Inuit culture is fascinated by these spirits, and many Inuit artists still make carvings of the *tupilak,* or spirits.

Sharing the Whale

When Inuit hunted together, the shaman would join in. Inuit believed that even the tupilak took part. In the case of some animals, such as whales, many hunters were needed to join the chase.

The more important the animal was for food, the more ritual was associated with the hunt. Meat and skin from large animals were shared according to who threw the first harpoon or who owned the umiak or sledge. A large whale might provide enough meat for several families, so a successful umiak owner was respected by the whole community. Nowadays most Inuit hunters use rifles and motorized vehicles to hunt, but many still follow traditional rituals of the hunt.

Below: This ancient pile of stones is called an *inukshuk,* which means "like a person." Inukshuks were probably first built by Dorset people.

Inukshuks helped mark routes across the Arctic, which has few natural landmarks. Rows of inukshuks were also set up near river crossings to direct caribou toward ambushes (hidden traps). At the ambush, hunters lay in wait to shoot the caribou. Hunters had to be careful not to upset the caribou spirits or to break taboos.

Above: Traditional stories and customs were passed on by word of mouth rather than in writing. During the long winter nights, parents would tell their children tales to teach them about their culture's beliefs and rituals. They also played games with their children to sharpen the young people's skills and natural reflexes. The children above are learning string games from their grandmother.

USE AND ABUSE OF THE ARCTIC

Until about 200 years ago, Inuit had no contact with the outside world. The Arctic way of life began to change when explorers first arrived there in the early 1800s. The explorers and whalers who came to the Arctic returned home with stories of seas full of whales. Products such as whale oil, which was used for lamp oil, were highly valued at that time.

European and North American merchants were eager to trade with the people of the Arctic. The merchants exchanged tea, tobacco, and other goods for furs provided by Native peoples. The traders brought new products, ideas, and religions. But they also brought diseases to which Native peoples had never been exposed. Since Native peoples had no resistance to the diseases, thousands died from illnesses such as measles and tuberculosis. The traders also brought alcohol. They found that they could make better bargains with Native hunters who had drunk alcohol. Over the years, Native peoples have struggled with the harmful effects of alcohol. In some areas, drinking alcohol is now restricted.

Arctic waters provided many whales, but whalers killed so many that the animals became scarce. Whalers began trading furs instead, relying on the hunting and trapping skills of indigenous peoples.

For awhile the fur trade brought jobs and money to Native peoples in the Arctic. But European fur markets were unreliable. Prices rose and fell dramatically, bringing short periods of prosperity followed by times of terrible hardship for Arctic hunting communities.

Right: The right whale got its name because whalers from North America and Europe considered the animal the right kind of whale to catch. It floated when dead and provided tons of oil and long sheets of **baleen** (whalebone) for making buggy whips, corsets, and fishing rods.

Below: Nowadays most Inuit in Canada live in settlements, such as this one at Igloolik, Northwest Territories.

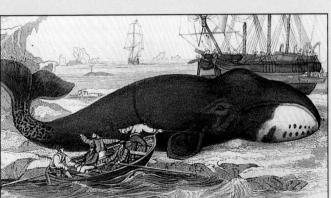

A SETTLED LIFE

During the 1900s, more outsiders than ever before have come to the Arctic. They have brought with them all the values and technology of the modern industrial world. As a result, the lifestyles and traditions of Native peoples in the Arctic have changed dramatically.

Hunters onced lived in one-room turf houses. They had no space or use for unnecessary possessions. Their sledges and harpoons were all that they required.

Nowadays many indigenous people in the Arctic live in small settlements. They have comfortable modern homes and schools. They shop in stores and receive health care at modern medical centers. Regular airplane flights provide transportation to other settlements and to cities in the south. Young people receive regular schooling and have more choices over their future.

As health care and housing have improved, the Native population in the Arctic has grown quickly. Not enough jobs are available for everyone. To help reduce unemployment in the North American Arctic, the U.S.

Above: The food and manufactured products in this store in Arctic Canada are shipped from industrial countries. Historically Inuit did not have processed food. Some Inuit feel they are betraying their traditional culture by eating it.

Below: Snowmobiles are much faster than sled dogs. Although snowmobiles make transportation easy and fast, they have also made the Arctic a much noisier place to live.

Above: Helicopters bring supplies, mail, and even doctors to the remotest parts of the Arctic. This helicopter is landing at a settlement in Greenland. Governments in the Arctic help pay for part of the cost of the flights because they are so expensive to operate.

and Canadian governments have helped many communities set up fishing and craft co-operatives. Here Inuit sell soapstone carvings and other arworks, which are popular with tourists.

Some indigenous people in the Arctic have found jobs in the oil and mining industries. Yet many still preserve the old ways. Some families maintain a hunting lifestyle on the land for at least part of the year.

Changing from the old ways to the new has not been easy. Many Arctic peoples are working to keep alive their languages, traditional skills, culture, and sense of community. Young people of the next generations will be challenged to find a balance between their traditional culture and the conveniences of modern life.

Above: Before Inuit had rifles, they tracked their prey with harpoons, knives, and bows. To kill the animals, hunters had to get very close to the animals and risked being badly wounded. Rifles have changed the hunting way of life dramatically by tipping the balance in the hunters' favor. They can shoot accurately from farther away and are more likely to kill their prey.

WEALTH OF THE ARCTIC

The Arctic is rich in coal and other minerals. But with few roads, it is difficult and expensive to transport minerals across the Arctic to industrial cities of the south. Companies will mine coal in areas of the Arctic where sea ice melts in summer. Then ships can load and transport the cargo. But some mines, such as the coal mines on Spitsbergen, are in completely uninhabited areas where no one has ever lived. The wildlife and natural wilderness in these places have all been changed by mining.

Making Way for Mining

Valuable minerals such as gold, copper, and nickel have been found and mined in the Arctic. Vast fields of oil and

Left: A long pipeline was built across Alaska in the 1970s to transport oil and natural gas. In some cases, the pipeline cuts across caribou migration routes. In others it divides traditional Native hunting grounds. The pipeline cost a lot to build. During construction the tundra and forests were damaged.

NATIVE LANGUAGES

As Europeans and other outsiders settled in the Arctic, they used their languages to communicate with indigenous peoples in the region. As a result, fewer and fewer Arctic peoples speak their own languages.

As in other communities, Arctic peoples have many words to describe the land. The Inuit, for example, use dozens of words to describe different types of ice. Most Arctic languages have been in written form for only 150 years.

Some Arctic languages are spoken in several countries. For example, **Yupik** is spoken from eastern Siberia to Alaska. **Inuktitut** is used in Canada and in Greenland. A variety of languages are spoken in Russia. The Sami and the Nenet, for example, would not understand each other.

natural gas have also been discovered. Many of these fields are found along the edges of the Arctic Ocean and underneath its icy waters. These deposits of oil and gas are important to both North America and Russia.

Mining and oil exploration in the Arctic have generally been more organized than exploration for gold. Only very large companies can afford to search for minerals, build mines, or drill oil wells in the faraway, frozen lands of the Arctic.

Aboriginals have not always had a say in who owns and profits from the natural resources of their traditional homelands. Many have been moved off their lands so that mining companies can explore and drill. This is changing slowly as Native groups begin to negotiate with governments for more control of the land and its resources.

The Arctic Experience

Nowadays tourists pay a lot of money to visit the Arctic. Many come to camp or hike in the Arctic wilderness. Others want to see whales, seals, or the region's vast bird colonies. Some tourists come to visit northern settlements. But people must be careful to protect the Arctic treasures that tourists come to see. For example, visitors arrive when many animals are breeding. If the trips are not carefully managed, the wildlife will be disrupted.

Left: Much of the Nenet people's traditional herding land has been taken over to build oil and gas rigs, such as the one in the background. After the 1917 revolution in Russia, the Russian government forced prisoners to work in the Arctic. They lived in labor camps and soon outnumbered the Native population.

29

MILITARY BUILDUP

Various nations became interested in the Arctic in the early 1900s, when the region's mineral wealth was discovered. Canada, for example, organized and sent police forces to control the whalers, trappers, and traders in the far north. For the first time, Native peoples in the Canadian Arctic had to live by a system of law very different from their own. The Canadian government prevented some Native practices. Native people gradually came to realize that outsiders sometimes considered them an inferior group of people.

Police posts were a sign of Canada's control over Arctic lands. Native ownership was ignored. In some cases, families were later moved from the land to settled communities.

The governments of countries surrounding the Arctic Ocean argued over boundaries. Military bases were built

Above: Iqaluit on Baffin Island in northern Canada is a thriving community and government center. The settlement grew up around an airfield that was an important refueling station during World War II.

Right: Many parts of the Arctic are littered with abandoned military bases and aircraft. The cost of cleaning up is high, and governments do not want to spend the money. Aboriginal peoples sometimes gather scrap metal and other materials from these abandoned sites.

Above: Airfields and military bases were built on Greenland, Spitsbergen, and in the Canadian Arctic during World War II. Greenland and Spitsbergen were important military sites because shipping routes passed close by.

to protect borders, but Aboriginal peoples were not consulted.

The Cold War

Military activity in the Arctic increased during World War II (1939–1945) and during the period of international tension known as the **Cold War,** which followed the war. For awhile many people were worried that another world war would be launched over the Arctic. So the United States built a line of radar stations across the Arctic, stretching from Alaska to Greenland. This line of defense was called the **Distant Early Warning (DEW) Line.** The DEW Line has been rebuilt several times. Each time the waste from the old radar stations was just left behind.

Some Inuit got jobs helping build and run the military bases. Families were attracted by regular wages, and they settled in communities. Similar radar stations were built across Russia, but government secrecy was greater there than in North America. Native peoples had little contact with the bases and were banned from using nearby land.

Military bases were also built on large pieces of sea ice. These floating ice stations gave scientists the first chance to study the Arctic Ocean in detail.

THE VALUE OF THE ARCTIC

The peoples of the Arctic see themselves as part of a
large environment made up of the land and its
animals and plants. Indigenous peoples have found
a way to live in the north, making an art of surviving
the harsh climate and long winter nights. Inuit have
developed one of the world's most distinctive
cultures. Historically Inuit relied on little more than
the meat, skin, bones, and blubber of the animals
they hunted. But it was a hard life. Nowadays many
Inuit struggle to balance the ease and luxury of life
in modern settlements with their cultural traditions.
Some people give up the old ways, hoping to find
happiness in a new lifestyle.

Right: An Inuk waits
patiently with his
harpoon at a seal's
breathing hole in
Greenland. The
knowledge and values of
Arctic peoples cannot be
measured in dollars.
Their skills have
developed over
thousands of years. If
these skills are lost, they
would be hard to replace.

Meanwhile, outside governments and large
companies tend to see the Arctic as a source of
profit. But many people—Native peoples and
outsiders alike—value the Arctic for its wilderness,
wildlife, and natural beauty. To Native peoples, and
to people lucky enough to have traveled to the
Arctic, the region has a value beyond money.

Right: A Nenet woman in Russia
harnesses a reindeer. The lifeways of
Nenet herders are changing quickly.
Mining companies are taking over
traditional herding lands. To control
the land and its resources, governments
often try to prevent Native peoples
from following their nomadic lifestyles.

Above: Meat and sealskins dry on a rack in northwestern Greenland. Historically Inuit have survived winters by storing food in summer, when there are plenty of seals and other animals to hunt.

RICHES OF THE ARCTIC SEAS

The seas of the Arctic are some of the richest in the world. The shallow bays of the islands along the coast of the Arctic Ocean are perfect places for plankton and fish to breed and grow. Masses of nutrients (materials that nourish living things) are released when the sea ice melts in spring. The nutrients allow billions of tiny animals and plants to breed. Seals and migrating whales rely on this food supply each year. Native peoples in Arctic Alaska have long hunted bowhead whales,

Below: Gulls flock around a small fishing boat off the coast of Newfoundland in Canada. In this area, the cold water of the Arctic Ocean mixes with the warmer water of the Atlantic Ocean. This mixing of water brings up nutrients from the bottom of the ocean. The amount of fish caught by crews on both big and little fishing boats, which work in shallow seas near coastlines, is carefully controlled.

Above: Eider ducks and a pair of snow geese (center) rest at the edge of an ice floe in Greenland. A few types of birds, such as ptarmigan and snowy owls, spend the winter in the Arctic. Most others migrate to the Arctic to breed and then leave in the fall. Scientists estimate that one million eiders alone pass the north coast of Alaska during each migration.

Above: The ringed seal is one source of food for the Inuit. These animals live on coastal ice, which makes them easy prey for hunters. About six or seven million ringed seals live in the Arctic.

which pass near the coast during their spring migration to the Beaufort Sea.

Overhunting and Overfishing

European and North American whalers hunted so many whales in the 1800s and early 1900s that the sea mammals were almost killed off. The population of Arctic whales has never fully recovered from this slaughter. Several types of whales are still in danger of extinction. In the 1980s, the International Whaling Commission (IWC) placed a moratorium (temporary halt) on commercial whaling. Several countries, however, do not pay attention to the moratorium and continue to catch whales commercially.

The IWC allows Native peoples in the Arctic to hunt whales for food. This is because whaling is a traditional, historic practice and is part of the culture of Native Arctic peoples. Nowadays Inuit use guns to hunt whales from motorized boats. Hunting is strictly controlled, and each community is licensed to catch only a certain number of whales each year.

For years, fishing fleets from Europe, North America, and Japan have fished Arctic waters, hauling in millions of tons of fish each year. In some areas, fish are caught faster than they can reproduce. Nations around the world have agreed to reduce net sizes and to restrict fishing to give fish stocks a chance to rebuild their populations.

BALANCING THE WEATHER

The polar regions play an important role in determining the world's weather. The ice caps and cold oceans cool the air and cause weather systems to sweep out onto surrounding lands. Currents from the Arctic Ocean flow past the coast of Greenland, bringing cold water and icebergs into the seas off North America, Asia, and Europe. The size of Arctic glaciers and ice caps has changed over time as the climate has grown warmer or colder. During the ice ages, the ice caps came as far south as central North America, Europe, and Russia.

Right: On a cold winter day, cracks in the sea ice freeze rapidly. The cracks give off **sea smoke,** just like the "smoke" that forms when a person blows breath out on a chilly day. Sea ice is always moving. Cracks open and close as wind and ocean currents move the ice around. Camping on sea ice can be dangerous. Some Inuit hunters travel hundreds of miles each year across the ice, looking for seals and polar bears.

Scientific Study of the Ice

Many scientists believe that the ice in the Arctic will provide the first clues of any changes in the earth's climate. For example, tree rings show what the weather was like in the past. But trees do not live a long time. Snowfall in the Arctic varies between summer and winter, and layers of snow can be counted just like tree rings. The Greenland ice cap is about two miles (three kilometers) thick. Scientists have drilled deep into the ice cap to collect **ice cores.** By counting the layers and measuring the chemicals in the ice cores, scientists can see what the weather was like thousands of years ago.

Arctic science has become so important that groups such as the Arctic Sciences Committee have formed to discuss and agree on international scientific studies. Large projects costing millions of dollars have examined the thickness of ice on land and at sea.

Above: The **northern lights** are the greatest natural show on earth. They occur during electrical storms high in the sky, almost at the edge of the atmosphere. This spectacular display was photographed over northern Norway.

Below: A group of scientists set up an ice camp high on the ice cap of Greenland. The group is studying the ice, which is about two miles (three kilometers) thick. By drilling deep holes into the ice, the scientists learn what the weather was like thousands of years ago.

THE FUTURE OF THE ARCTIC

Over time natural events have brought about many changes in the Arctic. Ice ages have covered the region in ice, and seas have dried up. But nowadays humans have the power to change the Arctic in dramatic ways. Many people realize that human activities can harm the environment. We often hear or read about the damage caused to rain forests and to rivers. But few people know that the Arctic is also threatened.

Human activities can harm the Arctic in two ways. Some damage is the result of what people do within the Arctic. For example, whaling in the 1800s and early 1900s nearly killed off some types of whales and other animals. On the other hand, some damage is caused by what people do outside the Arctic. Pollution from North America, Europe, and Asia is spreading into the Arctic. Most scientists believe certain human activities are warming the earth's climate. But nobody knows for sure how this warming might affect Arctic ice caps, glaciers, and the lives of Arctic peoples.

Right: Large rivers flow northward across Russia and Asia into the Arctic Ocean. The waterways carry important nutrients and millions of tons of fresh water to the Arctic. Planners wanted to direct these rivers southward to irrigate, or water, farmland in Central Asia. If the project had not been dropped, the wildlife and sea waters of Russia's Arctic coastline would have suffered.

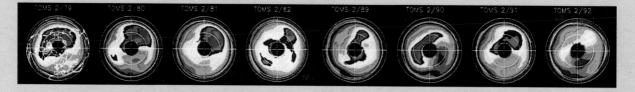

This color scale shows areas of low total ozone in blue or purple. Areas of high total ozone are red or green.

Above: **Ozone** is a chemical that naturally forms high in the earth's atmosphere. Ozone helps protect the earth from the harmful rays in sunlight. If ozone disappeared, the skin of humans, animals, and plants would burn badly.

Each year humans use tons of manufactured chemicals. Some of them, such as **chlorofluorocarbons** (or CFCs), rise into the upper atmosphere, where they destroy ozone. The pictures above show changes in the amount of ozone in recent years. Arctic peoples suffer when the ozone level is low. The sun's harmful rays can cause partial blindness or skin cancers in people who do not wear protective clothing. In 1990 the United States and 80 other nations agreed to stop making CFCs by the year 2000.

THREATS TO THE ARCTIC

Nowadays growing industries are the main threat to the Arctic. International mining companies search for oil and gas in northern territories. The Canadian and Russian governments, for example, have paid mining companies a lot of money to explore Arctic lands. For thousands of years, Prudhoe Bay on the north coast of Alaska was visited only by Native hunters. Nowadays thousands of people work there for the oil industry. Some of these workers are Native Arctic peoples. Earning regular wages allows a more secure lifestyle than relying only on hunting.

The machinery needed to operate oil wells is brought into the Arctic by ship during summer. Some of the oil is then transported by huge tankers to refineries. Cargo ships and icebreakers, which plow easily through sea ice, are common in Lancaster Sound in the Canadian Arctic. They bring supplies for oil wells and mines. Nobody knows exactly what effect shipping has on seabirds, seals, and whales, or on the Aboriginals who rely on these animals.

The Oil Industry

How would Aboriginal hunters be affected if a huge tanker spilled its cargo of oil? Scientists are still studying the environmental damage caused by the 1989 oil spill of the *Exxon Valdez* oil tanker in Alaska. Much of the

Above: Drilling for oil and natural gas has affected the peoples and the environment of the Arctic. Hundreds of years may go by before the slow-growing plants of the Arctic cover these tracks across the tundra of the Yamal Peninsula in northwestern Russia. Few areas are damaged like this, but more industries are moving to the Arctic every year. New parks and refuges are being established to help limit the threat to Arctic animals and plants as well as to Native peoples.

Above: The oil and natural gas industry provides jobs and good wages for many people in Arctic communities. But hunting grounds and herding routes have been disturbed by building oil and gas wells.

Left: Explorers, soldiers, and industrial workers have left waste all over the Arctic. In cold, dry Arctic conditions, metal containers such as these fuel drums on Melville Peninsula in Canada, rust very slowly. The drums are ugly to look at, but the cost of cleanup is high. On the other hand, local people sometimes rely on the military dumps for scrap metal.

Arctic's oil is brought out in pipelines, too. But pipelines are not completely safe. And building pipelines has caused damage to the tundra (see page 28).

Global Warming

Several threats to the environment of the Arctic come from outside the region. Chemicals that have never been used in the Arctic have been found in some of the region's birds and fish. Winds and ocean currents bring this pollution into the Arctic from industrial centers outside the area. **Global warming** is an even bigger problem. Many scientists think that burning oil and other fossil fuels is warming the planet. But no one knows exactly how warm it would have to be for the Arctic and Antarctic ice caps to melt. If they do melt, sea levels will rise and many areas will be flooded. Nobody can tell what would happen to Arctic weather if the sea ice melted.

ARCTIC CHOICES

Very few people live in the Arctic. Ever since the first explorers and whalers arrived in the region, outsiders have tried to pass on their culture to the Native peoples of the Arctic. In some cases, Native children were sent to schools where they learned new religions and new languages, far from their families.

Some changes have been helpful. Medical workers have brought modern medicines and techniques to the Arctic to help reduce the number of children who die and to help cure diseases. As a result, many northern groups have larger populations than ever before. Most Native Arctic youth go to school regularly. Their languages, once completely oral, now have written alphabets so information can be recorded in books.

When Native teenagers see fast snowmobiles and fashionable goods, they often want to buy them. But many elders believe their cultural traditions, which are not based on material items, are disappearing. Nowadays Native peoples have more choices in how they live and work. But indigenous people do not always get the best jobs—sometimes because these jobs are not available and sometimes because workers lack specific job skills.

Native peoples use many things that make life easier. They use television and radio, for example, to communicate with others and to share ideas about working with government. Although guns now make hunting easier, Aboriginals control the number of animals they hunt in order to preserve wildlife for the future.

Wildlife Refuges

More people are living in the Arctic, which is developing quickly. Aboriginals, along with scientists and conservationists, have helped persuade governments to keep areas protected for wildlife. As a result of these efforts, parks and refuges have been established.

But in some cases, a park may not be safe from development. For example, the Porcupine Caribou Herd spends the winter in Canada's Yukon. In spring the caribou migrate into Alaska to feed and bear their young in the Arctic National Wildlife Refuge. But oil companies want to explore the refuge for oil. Many Canadian and U.S. citizens are working hard to prevent mining in the Alaskan refuge.

Right: Native peoples are working to protect wildlife from overhunting. In some areas, such as Thule in northwest Greenland, Inuit collect the eggs of eider ducks on only two days each year. This has given the animals a better chance of reproducing, and the number of eider ducks is increasing. But even though birds may be protected in their Arctic breeding grounds, they still risk being shot when they migrate to other lands.

Below: Protecting animals in one country would be useless if they were shot as soon as they crossed the border. So scientists from different countries have worked together to persuade governments to protect Arctic wildlife across international boundaries. Polar bears, for example, travel over the sea ice from Russia to Greenland or to Canada. Conservationists from several countries persuaded their governments to protect the bears, whose population is now increasing.

PEOPLE POWER

Until recently many governments have treated the Arctic as though nobody lived there. Governments have issued licences for whaling, fur trading, and mining without consulting Native peoples.

As industries developed in the Arctic, Native peoples began to realize that their way of life was vanishing. To help protect their cultures and traditions, they formed Native groups. These groups questioned the right of

Above: Each year more people visit the Arctic. They come to see glaciers and wildlife, or to experience traveling by dogsled or by kayak. These tourists admire the beautiful glaciers in Magdalene Fjord in Spitsbergen.

#2
Chinook

the
Tundra
Buggy

governments to give industries permission to build on what Native peoples believed was their land. As more oil wells and pipelines were built across the Arctic, Native groups confronted large companies and governments. In 1971 Alaskan Native groups made an agreement with the U.S. government for money and control of some of the land.

This success encouraged other groups to challenge their governments' actions. In 1977 the first Inuit Circumpolar Conference was held. The conference brought together Native groups from many countries of the Arctic. This large group has been successful in challenging exploration and mining on traditional Native lands. And in 1992 the Inuit of northern Canada were successful in establishing Nunavut—a new territory where Inuit will have self-government and will be able to make decisions about mining in their territory.

Above: A tourist in Norway takes a picture of a group of Sami in traditional dress.

Left: Polar bears are curious. This one is inspecting tourists at Cape Churchill, Canada.

The Future of the Land
Native Arctic peoples may never have complete control over the land because the region's natural resources are so important to the economies of powerful international nations. Many people feel that fishing, mining, and other uses of the land must be managed carefully to protect the environment for the future. As Native peoples continue the struggle for more control of their lands, the future of the Arctic will be in the hands of those who have cared for it for the last 3,000 years.

Glossary

angákoq: The Inuit word for healers, or shamans. An angákoq helps Inuit maintain contact with the spirit world, which they believe inhabits animals, plants, and land.

Antarctica: The continent surrounding the South Pole.

Arctic: The region surrounding the North Pole. The Arctic includes the Arctic Ocean and part of the surrounding continents.

Arctic Circle: A line on a globe or map that circles the northern polar region at about the 66th degree of northern latitude. All places north of the Arctic Circle have at least one 24-hour period each year when the sun does not set.

baleen: Thin plates of material similar to human fingernails that hang in the mouths of some large whales. The whales use these plates to strain out the small animals they feed on in the sea.

blubber: A layer of fat below the skin of whales and seals that insulates, or protects, the animals from the cold.

caribou: A large type of deer that lives in large herds in the forests and on the tundra of North America.

chlorofluorocarbons (CFCs): Manufactured chemicals used in refrigerators, plastic foams, cleaning fluids, and air-conditioning systems. CFCs can damage the ozone layer of the earth's upper atmosphere.

Cold War: The period of tension between the democratic countries of North America and Western Europe and the Communist countries of the Soviet Union and Eastern Europe. The Cold War lasted from the end of World War II until the late 1980s. Both sides built up large military forces in case of war.

Distant Early Warning (DEW) Line: A series of radar stations built across the Arctic by the United States in the 1950s to give early warning of a missile attack.

equator: A line on a map that circles the earth at 0° of latitude. The equator lies at an equal distance from the North Pole and the South Pole.

extinction: The complete dying out of a species of animal, either from natural causes or from overhunting by people.

glacier: A huge, slow-moving mass of ice and snow that moves slowly down mountain valleys.

global warming: A rise in the average temperature of the earth's atmosphere. Many scientists believe the warming is caused by a buildup of carbon dioxide and other gases in the air.

harpoon: A long, pointed weapon resembling a spear. Used by Inuit hunters to catch seals and whales, harpoons have barbed heads and are attached to a line.

Ice Age: A period when ice caps cover large regions of the earth. The term *Ice Age* usually refers to the most recent one, called the Pleistocene, which began almost 2 million years ago and ended about 10,000 years ago.

ice cap: A huge mass of ice and snow that covers large areas of a continent. Antarctica, on the South Pole, has the largest ice cap on earth. Greenland has the largest ice cap in the Arctic.

ice core: A large sample of ice that is drilled out from deep in the interior of an ice cap. By examining ice cores, scientists can learn about the weather conditions that existed thousands of years ago.

iceberg: A very large mass of ice that breaks off from a glacier near the sea and floats away slowly in the water.

inukshuk: A pillar of stones originally built by ancient Arctic hunters to guide travelers across the region or to lead caribou into an ambush. From a distance, an inukshuk looks something like a person.

Inuktitut: An Arctic language spoken by the Inuit in Canada and Greenland.

kayak: A small, one-person boat traditionally used for hunting seals and small whales. Nowadays kayaks are also a popular recreational boat.

latitude: A line circling a globe or map. The equator circles the middle of the earth at 0° of latitude and lies at an equal distance from the North Pole and the South Pole.

lichen: A plant made up of algae and fungus growing together on solid surfaces, such as rocks, trees, or poor-quality soil.

longitude: A line on a map or globe that runs from the North Pole to the South Pole. The zero line (0° of longitude) runs through Greenwich in London, England.

mammal: A member of a large group of warm-blooded animals (including humans), in which the females feed their young on their own milk.

migration: Regular, seasonal journeys from one territory to another by people or animals searching for fresh pastures or hunting grounds.

missionary: A person sent out by a religious group to spread its beliefs to other people.

moss: A small plant with a leafy, tufted stem. Mosses usually grow in tightly packed clusters on damp surfaces.

nomadic lifestyle: A way of life in which people do not have permanent dwellings. They travel from place to place within a territory, often to make the best use of seasonal foods and other natural resources.

northern lights: Also known as aurora borealis, these streaks of colored light are seen in the night sky in northern parts of the world. Scientists think the lights are caused by particles from the sun hitting the outer parts of the earth's atmosphere.

ozone: A form of oxygen that is produced naturally in the earth's atmosphere. Ozone protects living creatures on earth from the harmful rays of the sun.

pack ice: Large masses of ice that form when sea ice breaks up in the spring.

permafrost: Ground that stays frozen year-round. A thin layer of surface soil thaws during the spring and summer, but the ground below remains frozen.

plankton: A mass of tiny animals and plants that floats in the sea and provides food for larger marine animals.

Sami (Lapps): A people of northern Scandinavia, Finland, and Russia. Traditionally the Sami lived a nomadic lifestyle herding reindeer, hunting sea mammals, and fishing.

sea smoke: Water vapor that looks like smoke and is caused by warm air meeting cooler air as cracks in sea ice freeze over.

sinew: A tough, flexible tissue or tendon that joins muscles to bones.

snowhouse: A dome-shaped house made from blocks of snow. The Inuit traditionally built snowhouses as temporary shelters when traveling.

tree line: The point north of which the climate is too cold and dry for trees to grow. Many scientists consider the tree line to be the southernmost limit of the Arctic region.

tundra: The flat, treeless plains of the Arctic. The only plants that can live on the tundra are small and grow close to the ground for protection from harsh winds.

tupilak: An evil spirit. The Inuit traditionally made carvings of the spirit to cast spells on enemies.

umiak: Large sealskin boats traditionally used by Inuit for hunting whales in summer. Crews of eight to ten people, often women, rowed the boats.

Yupik: An Arctic language spoken by peoples from eastern Siberia to Alaska.

Index